Index

Forward

This is a book I wish I could have read when I was in college at the University of New Haven in the mid 80's.

My goal is to not just help young adults land their dream job but help them discover what they love to do for a career.

Back in the 80's, there were only a few colleges that offered a version of Sports Management degree. It was not considered a traditional business from a higher education standpoint.

Especially one that you would go to college to study.

So upon graduation, like a lot of my friends and teammates, I wasn't sure what types of jobs were available in sports other than coaching or scouting.

Sports Management was just becoming a college major the year I graduated. Our school offered an intro class, but mostly just a concentration within business schools.

I believe Ohio University and UMASS were the first U.S. colleges to offer Sports Management as a degree.

In the 80's, coaching, broadcasting, or general management seemed to be the only way in and you had to know someone.

The business of sports wasn't even recognized by the outside world, including higher education, as a real global industry. Even though it was bigger than the auto industry.

Today not only is the global sports industry thriving, so is the higher educational platforms that promise that entry point.

There are roughly 640+ sports management undergraduate and graduate degrees available at North American Universities.

An estimated $1 Billion was spent on sports management degrees in 2016 alone.

There is not a shortage of students and families who are investing in the traditional educational process to fulfill their dream to work in sports. However, there is a shortage of jobs for individuals who have the necessary skills and experience valued by sports organizations including: Teams, Leagues, Media Groups, Event and Activation Agencies, and National Governing Bodies.

There seems to be a disconnect with recent graduates who are struggling to land sports jobs right out of college.

It takes on average five years to land that first full-time sports job. Many give up and settle outside the industry.

There are several reasons why graduates can't land a job right out of school.

Graduates are not sure where to start or where they fit in. Having limited relationships with key sports organizations and limited necessary soft skills.

I wrote this book as a quick guide to provide the practical advice on the required skills necessary to not only land a job but have a long career in the sports industry.

Introduction

Let's face it, who didn't grow up wanting to work in sports for your favorite team that you used to root for, win or lose? The players became our heroes and a focal part of most of our young and adult lives.

Chances are your dad or your grandfather had a favorite team that you rooted for as a family. It was always part of your family, it was part of your culture. That passion is woven into the fabric of family entertainment.

With the explosion of video games, access to online merchandise, and fantasy sports, our passion has become fueled not only as a fan but as a participant. Video games allow us to become our favorite players and compete with someone sitting next to us in our living rooms, or in other parts of the world.

The ability to be immersed into the emotional connection to our favorite team is seamless and at our fingertips.

You imitate your favorite player with your clothes, music, and playing style.

You wanted to become a part of that team and in some ways today, you can digitally.

Working in sports has become an obsession for hundreds of thousands because it doesn't seem so impossible anymore. You don't have to be a former athlete or coach to become a general manager or a broadcaster. And everyone has a legit shot if you can only figure out how.

When people ask you, "What you do for a living," how cool would it be to tell them proudly, "I work for the New York Yankees. It's my favorite team and a job I've always wanted."

The great thing about that is it is reality for a lot of people. You may think of it as unattainable, but it isn't. If you're willing to be patient and hang in there, anything is achievable if your effort and talent matches your career goals.

It may not be a direct line.

It may not be your first job out of school.

It may take you 10 years to get there.

It may take some people 10 months or 10 days to get there.

Everybody's path is very different.

Everybody's journey is different.

If you don't start now, you'll never get there.

Chapter 1
Landing A Dream Job

I have been hosting a podcast show since 2015 where I interview entrepreneurs and executives in the sports industry.

I have interviewed plenty of famous agents, college athletic directors, pro athletes, team executives, commissioners, and many startup founders. One of my favorite podcast guests was with Steve Hogan, CEO of Florida Citrus Sports.

FCS is a non-for-profit community organization that hosts the Florida Citrus Bowl, Buffalo Wild Wing Bowl, Camping World Stadium Bowl, and the NFL Pro Bowl.

Mr. Hogan shared great stories about his first job in sports and how young professionals can take a similar path, which is not always a straight line.

This is Steve Hogan's story.

When Steve graduated from University of Central Florida as a former student athlete (Football) with a communication and journalism major, he did not have a job in sports.

His first full time job was selling cell phones to businesses and government agencies.

After a few years, he started selling advertising for a local newspaper group in the Orlando area.

He was calling on grocery stores, automobile agencies, cell phone companies, mom-and-pop shops, hair salons, gyms, etc. Anyone that he could get to advertise in the paper. He was really good at his job.

However, he really didn't like what he was doing. In fact, he hated it. The thought of getting up everyday to sell newspaper ads was as he put it, "Making me sick."

He knew he needed a change. He tapped into his network of friends and family for help and started asking them who they might know in sports organizations around Orlando.

Come to find out, his aunt knew someone at Florida Citrus Sports, and he got a meeting.

His meeting was with the CEO of the Citrus Bowl at the time, who gave him a shot with an entry level position to prove himself.

Steve was so excited about getting that opportunity to work in sports. He was going to take advantage of the opportunity, no matter the role.

What he didn't know at the time was that he was getting the opportunity to put his experience in sales to good use.

He found this out on his first day when he was handed a box of files. His role would be to sell sponsorships for the Citrus Bowl Parade.

At first, he thought, "What did this have to do with sports and the Bowl game?" But the lesson he learned was that even though it wasn't the game, it was a huge part of the overall fan experience for alums flying in for the weekend Bowl game.

This is where his previous experience in sales became valuable. He understood the art and science of selling. Over the past several years, he had built up tremendous relationships with local businesses which allowed him to hit the ground running on day one with the Citrus Bowl.

He embraced this opportunity so much that he quadrupled the revenue for the parade in his first year.

They hadn't seen that kind of sponsorship revenue at the Citrus Bowl Parade ever.

Steve went in and crushed it, which ultimately led them to have a great parade. Through tackling the current job with hard work, driving revenue, and exceeding what was asked, he moved up the promotional ladder. He built such a strong reputation inside the organization and within the business community that he eventually became the CEO of Florida Citrus Sports.

You never know what can happen when opportunities present themselves. Even if it doesn't seem to be in your game plan, each job is a building block on the foundation of your career.

Relationships, learning new skills, and exceeding expectations eventually will be your path to that dream job.

When Steve walked into the door that first day looking for an opportunity, he was given a box of files and a pat on the shoulder with a nice "Good Luck, here are the keys to the parade." He embraced the challenge and took it head on to exceed expectations.

Steve Hogan, after 20 plus years of leading Florida Citrus Sports, continues to exceed expectations and continues to be grateful for that opportunity so many years ago.

"It's difficult enough to get a job in sports. It's even harder to have a long career in sports." Steve Hogan

Chapter 2

My Story

I started my first business when I was 24 years old, newly married, just had our first child, and I saw an opportunity in high school athletics.

I believed high school football players in the Northeast were getting overlooked by college recruiters. Granted, you have to fish where the fish are, and some regions have a greater talent pool. But nonetheless, I felt like I had an obligation to help and saw an opportunity for a business.

When I was coaching college football at Boston University in 1990, there were limited, if any, recruiting services available. None of which were on the internet.

I saw the opportunity to provide a service and to help connect the dots between schools and prospects.

There were diamonds in the rough that were not getting discovered because of the limited resources available in the market for the fringe players.

In my opinion, there was a place for every kid that came out of high school who played football and sacrificed for four years or longer. There was a place for them to play somewhere in the United States, at any level, if they had the desire, talent, and attention.

A few things happened when I was coaching that lead me to understand the system.

While at BU, I was assigned to recruit Junior College prospects; "JUCO" players from California.

We happened to have a few players from the California JUCO's that had been great kids and players for us.

It made sense to go back there to mine a few more players, as we had already established a pipeline.

Although I was new to the staff and didn't have any relationships with JUCO coaches or even know any of the schools out there, I used my network of coaching to help make introductions.

I was given a name and number of a retired head coach who was originally from Rhode Island who eventually became the head coach and Athletic Director at Santa Barbara Community College. But was since retired.

With pure luck on my first call we spoke for nearly three hours and he was very happy to help me find players from California JUCO's whom he knew very well.

He was an old school Northeast Italian American coach, so needless to say, we hit it off immediately.

In typical Northeast fashion, he turned his garage into an office/kitchen/living room space overlooking the Pacific Ocean. This is where he spent most of his time watching film, smoking cigars, and drinking wine.

I had opportunities to go out and meet with him. Those long conversations with Coach were so valuable.

He was like Coach Gruden before his time. He had a rotation of college coaches that were passing through town that would always spend endless hours visiting with him in his garage. They would be breaking down film, telling stories, drinking amazing homemade wine, and eating Italian meats and cheeses, while sharing a nice cigar.

It had to be one of the best views in all of Santa Barbara. To us, it was a football coach's heaven.

What I saw Coach do as a one-stop-shop for college coaches, I thought if I ever left coaching, I would do the same thing.

So, in the Spring of 1991, I left college coaching and returned to Connecticut to marry my college sweetheart, start a family, and a new adventure.

That new adventure became the first high school football recruiting agency in the Northeast.

I certainly wasn't in a position to start a business. I didn't even know anything about business. I graduated from college in '89, played professional football in Europe, came back to the states, and coached college football.

I never had a real job other than working for a short time in a Juvenile Detention Facility.

And this was my real first step into the sports industry on the business side.

I was recently married, was ill prepared for any of this, but I just had a gut feeling that there was something out there that was needed in this space.

I had no idea about the business of sports other than playing or coaching.

After a year of starting the agency and having 200+ schools subscribe to my service, I merged with an agency that represented professional athletes.

Eventually the agency closed its doors after one of the partners went to jail. It was rather devastating but a life lesson.

I had to move on and went back to work at the Juvenile Detention Facility and started my own summer camps in my hometown. I was out of sports just like that. But I kept one foot in with a summer Oline-DLine camp and helping former college football players find teams to play on in Europe and Australia.

What eventually changed my professional life, is when I volunteered for a new youth initiative called, NFL Play Football Program. Which was the beginning of the NFL Flag football program.

In 1995, that program was launched with the New England Patriots in October of '94. I volunteered for the weekend to work at an NFL Flag Football camp in Biddeford, Maine.

It completely changed everything for me after that weekend. It gave me a little bit more of a sense of a purpose. I know I had that "aha" moment for what I wanted to be. I wanted to be apart of providing more opportunities for boys and girls to experience football in a non-contact, 5v5 fun way, without pads or complicated rules.

When I experienced what this initiative was about, I knew I wanted to be apart of it right then and there. Getting boys and girls, ages 6 - 14, to put a football in their hand and provide a vehicle to allow all kids from every corner of the world, regardless of ability or resources, to play football.

By volunteering without seeking anything in return, asking for nothing more than my time, it lead me down a path of a 7+ year journey throughout the world working for the NFL.

I met some amazing kids along the way that one weekend in which I had no intentions to do anything else but volunteer.

Our staff was sent to Biddeford, Maine, and meeting at that time, the new director of the NFL Youth Programs.

Him and I hit it off. Within a week after that weekend, I was on board with the NFL as the program consultant for the NFL Flag in the US.

I traveled all over the United States, Southeast Asia, Latin America, and Canada.

So I am what I now call an "accidental entrepreneur". Someone who discovered what he loved to do after going through bumps in the road and doing the things he didn't like to do.

Coming out of college, I didn't know how to get there, and starting my own business in the sports industry was definitely my first step to understanding how it all works and how cruel the world of business can be at times.

I thought it was the right thing to do. Ultimately getting hired by the NFL lead me on a journey with the Arena Football League, the Walt Disney Company, and eventually coming full circle to starting a sports marketing company; North American Sports Group.

When I look back on my journey, I think of the coach in Santa Barbara that I found by asking my network who they knew that could help me recruit California JUCO student athletes.

By simply volunteering one cold, rainy weekend in Maine and using the business opportunity I discovered in California, it launched my journey in the global sports industry.

"You will figure out what you hate doing, long before you discover a job you love, so try everything."

Chapter 3

The Real Deal

I hate to tell you this, but there are some harsh realities in the sports industry.

Like the expression that players and coaches use, NFL means Not-For-Long.

What they mean by that is it's not always about only talent, it's also very much about your attitude.

You need talent within your area of focus or position but your attitude when starting out is massively essential.

I learned a lesson at Disney that stays with me today. Hire nice, smart people, and train them. No one there ever said, "Only hire Ivy League level, smart people."

There are a lot of smart people. But can you get along with others and are you willing to do things not in your job description? Are you willing to come into work early, work late, work holidays and weekends? Are you willing to embark on low budget travel, get dirty, be tired, thirsty, hungry, and broke?

If the answer is yes, then the sports industry is for you.

Chances are you won't be hanging with the players or the coaches. You probably won't see any of the games live. You'll be working on operating the event and making sure the guests are having a great time.

You will work very, very long hours. Especially during the season.

You will not get paid enough or at least you're not getting paid enough. If you start counting how many hours you work in relation to your compensation, it's over.

When you start thinking that way, it could be that you feel that you're undervalued, underpaid, or underappreciated. But this is the business at the start.

Why? Because there are thousands of people willing and able to replace you.

Did I scare you a little?

My goal is not to make you change your mind, but rather help you understand the reality, manage your expectations, and prepare you to have the mindset to take on this incredible adventure.

As I mentioned before, you need to know that the path to your dream job is probably not going to be easy and perhaps one that is not directly in the industry at first. But if you know the relevant skill sets you need, you can transition over if you throw yourself 100% into wherever you are working.

Where do you start?

I talk a lot about the incredible advantage of the 95% of people in the world that have access to all the amazing technology and social media platforms.

So much in this business is rooted in attention. How do you create it, keep it, and repeat it?

In today's world, I believe that how well you understand creating, distributing, and analyzing digital media is the core of the business of sports and most industries.

Why? Because it's how we communicate and share content with fans, customers, clients, and future bosses. It's where there is the most attention.

But don't let that part make you freak out and start posting more. You need to understand the art and science of how it all works.

Your psychology classes are more important than you think to help you understand human behavior and the correlation on how social media is consumed.

We will get into this more in Chapter Five.

So where do you start in the business?

What are the things that you enjoy doing?

- Are you good with numbers and analytics?
- Are you an extrovert and don't have a problem talking to complete strangers and have a huge social media following?
- Do you have a blog, podcast, or vlog?
- Are you super creative and enjoy graphic design, website development, programming, or video editing?
- Are you very organized, love planning, a linear thinker, and need structure?
- Do you like to do physical work and are a "fix it" type person?
- Are you a stats and into eSports?

You need to know who you are first in order to focus on where you are heading.

I break the industry into three areas. There are many businesses that are attached, but for simplicity sake, I will stick with the core three.

First they are the leagues, governing bodies, and teams. Second, media and distribution platforms. Third, the agency's and vendors that support "The Event".

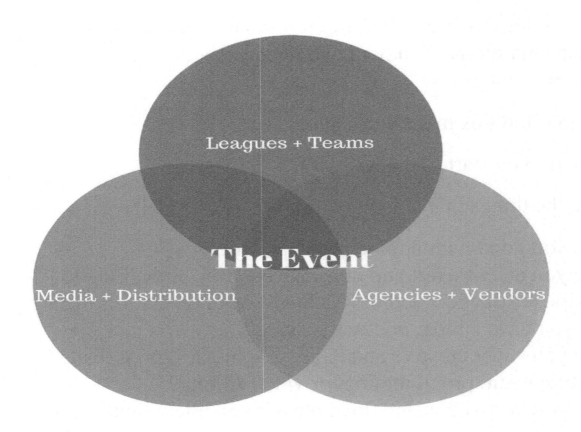

The important aspect to know is that in each circle there are positions in the core areas of Sales, Operations & Management.

Regardless if you work for a local ESPN Radio affiliate in sales or an agency that provides management of a grassroots tour for a USA Swimming sponsor, you are technically in the sports industry.

Starting off in sports with an inside sales position selling season tickets is not always the best fit.

It is one of the most readily available position and internships in sports and a tremendous way to get a foot in and learn the business. However, there is a high turnover rate because it's not for everyone and requires thick skin.

Unfortunately, it's a graveyard for many career seekers first taste in the business. They turn and burn after a season or a year. They get a job selling medical devices and after two years are bored and want back into the industry.

It usually doesn't happen and can be a red flag to another team.

I believe working on the agency or media side as a first job is a great place to learn what you like doing.

If you are more of the linear thinker, creative, hands on doer, rather than the extravert.

Agency and media departments are incredible jobs to explore to see what areas you like best. You will have the chance to work on multiple projects within an array of areas. It may be sports, music, culinary, travel, fashion, etc.

Working on P&L's, campaigns, activation tours, paid media, and content creation is a broad stroke of understanding how the sponsors leverage their relationships to properties.

The reality of my point in this chapter, is know yourself. Knowing yourself, being honest with yourself, and owning that honesty will put you in the best position to be really good at your job.

Know what you are good at, know what you hate doing, and go all in on what you love doing the most.

"There is no such thing as a bad decision in your career. Once you make the decision, make it your best."

Chapter 4

Immersion Into The Industry

Here are some fun facts.

There are 640+ universities that offer sports management, undergraduate, and graduate degrees in the United States.

In 2017, there was an estimated 30,000 graduates with sports management undergrad and graduate degrees.

However, there were only roughly 10,000 jobs that were publicly posted on job boards such as workinsports.com

55% of the jobs posted were entry level sales positions.

There was a 40% increase in social media sports jobs, yet less than 5% of degrees require social media, or sales courses.

On average, a four-year college sports management degree will cost $100,000. For many of you it will cost less with grants and academic scholarships.

Needless to say the investment in a degree is substantial and the competition for entry level positions are fierce.

What does this all mean? Experience.

How do you gain experience while you are going to school?

Your college sport management department and professors will provide you with opportunities via a job board or emails on local opportunities at minor league teams, rec facilities, agency's, etc.

If you go to a university that is NCAA D1, more than likely you will have plenty of opportunities to volunteer or work on campus games in multiple sports. Something you should seek out, especially if you are in High School and seeking the right fit.

If you are currently in High School, I highly recommend volunteering at local minor league teams, 5k's, YMCA's and any event that is happening at your school and in the community.

Volunteering is not only a great purpose but the learnings of how events are executed is the foundation of the industry. Being able to dip your toe in the water will give a sense of the amount of work and flow of the business before jumping in all the way committing to investing in a four year sport management degree.

As I have said before, try everything. Before you can become a celebrity chef on the food network, work in a really busy Olive Garden kitchen! See if you like it.

Try lots of things, volunteer every chance you get and explore as many aspects of the industry, regardless how small they are or unglamorous they may seem at the time.

Life experiences is knowledge.

Chapter 5

Multiple Skills

The mindset in today's world is multiple skill sets bring tremendous value to any business.

I put them into Five categories:

1) Content Creation
2) Content Production
3) Content Distribution
4) Content Analytics
5) Content Monetization

These are soft skills needed for today's entry level positions; Sales, Event Management, and Social Media Management.

The thinking behind that for employers is that access to learn how to do anything is always a google search away.

There is an assumption that if you are under the age of 30, chances are you know how to program, you know how to edit GOPRO videos, you can build a website, design fantastic graphics, create spreadsheets, and have 10,000 + followers on Instagram.

That may not be necessarily true in most cases, but if you do have many of those skills, it is a huge advantage to separate yourself from the pack.

Remember there were 30,000 graduates last year but there are only 6,000 publicly posted jobs.

There's a big discrepancy. The market place is crowded and very competitive for a very narrow amount of jobs that are available.

The relevant skills that you have are impactful, important, and deliver value to a business. It's not about where you received your education, rather, how you apply your skills.

Perhaps you have a master's degree or MBA. The relevant skills are definitely going to be the ones that get you past the finish line. They're going to get you a job.

The majority of entry level sports jobs are inside sales jobs. Over 55% of them are in ticket sales.

What does that mean to you if you don't like sales and are uncomfortable cold calling strangers?

Get comfortable with being uncomfortable. It clicks in when you feel a sense of helping people. When you get to provide them with great entertainment opportunities in their community.

For an entry level sales position, you need to have multiple skills that provide more value to a sports organization.

How to create a sales funnel, which is building a reputation and attention to you being the portal for friends, family, and fans to your team's assets such as tickets, hospitality, and sponsorships.

You will do this through cold calls, social media, and networking outside of work. Everyone you meet is a potential customer.

Awareness leads to conversation and interest, which then becomes converting into a customer.

Working with a CRM software, such as Salesforce, allows you to track contacts and communication. It also provides a guide to stay on course for follow up and closing business.

Do you understand "Social Selling"?

Social selling is prospecting clients and fans building a digital sales funnel from a business perspective with social media. Essentially building followers by providing them with informative content that brings your digital community value, humor, and inspiration.

Don't try to sell them on every post. Instead get them to like and trust you as an expert and the access point to the business you represent.

Do you know how to prospect search hashtags?

How updated is your LinkedIn account? This is the best channel to utilize.

Seek out executives on LinkedIn after you send your resume to that business. Follow that person on Twitter and Instagram. Engage with them on their post, get them to know who you are by posting great relevant content.

Recruiters and employers will look at your social media accounts, so unlock your Instagram.

If there are pictures on your IG you don't want grandma to see, delete them today.

If your account is still locked, chances are that will reflect in you being hired.

It's not that employers are interested in your personal life, they do want to see some, but they also want to see how you post and what copy you are writing to engage your audience.

If you are an active Instagram user and only have 200 followers, chances are you're not a good fit for sales.

Do you know how to build an online community? That is relevant experience for a sales position.

The realities of what is needed by teams are sales and revenue. The above is all tied to that critical objective regardless if it's college, minor league, or the pros.

You're selling tickets, customer service, premium seats, and sponsorship, which will require you to pick up the phone and cold call complete strangers.

You need to be comfortable with that, or you need to have experience coming into that, which will give you an advantage.

If you were doing inside or door to door sales for a lawn service, that's huge relevant experience that translates.

If you interned for an insurance agency and you were picking up the phone, dialing for dollars, lining up new appointments for the agents then it's all relevant.

As I mentioned before, you are going to need thick skin because you will be rejected the majority of the time.

From a social media standpoint, do you know how to prospect influencers for sales on social media?

Do you understand the backend of Facebook analytics and advertisement?

Do you know how many followers you have on your own channels? It is important because the more followers that you have, the more engaged you are, and that makes an employer believe you know what you're doing in that space.

So, there's a difference between your personal and the professional way to approach social media. There's an art and science behind it.

There's science behind what it takes to prospect influencers on Instagram and on Twitter.

How to connect with customers is where the business is headed. Knowing that skill and having the skill sets to be able to do that, to grow followers, will help you stand out.

Graphic design is another relevant skill set that is a huge value to a business.

How good are you at graphic design? Can you do presentations?

Can you create social media posts?

Can you create collateral?

Can you program a website?

Anything that has to do with content creation in the digital space is a huge advantage if you have it.

Canva.com, Upsplash.com, are both great free tools to use for graphic design if you are not great at Adobe software.

Do you have a popular blog, vlog, or podcast?

I started an iTunes podcast a few years ago, "The Business of Sports with Rob Thompson," and it gave me not only a voice, but it allows me to get in front of high level executives and interesting people in the industry.

I highly recommend podcasting. I use a free app called, Anchor.fm. It automatically uploads to iTunes and four other podcasting platforms.

Podcasting is amazing content and giving you a voice. That is important because AI is disrupting the market on how we will purchase and consume information.

Do you know how to edit short form video?

Short form video editing is a huge advantage as a skill set.

Can you create 3D digital renderings or animated videos?

Anything that could be used in highlights, anything that can be used in social media, anything that you use in Snaps, Instagram, and going live.

Being able to edit long and short form video is just one more relevant skill set that brings incredible value to a business and gives you another area to stand out in. You don't need to be an expert at editing but having the general ability to do so, if asked, is key.

And then the nucleus of the sports industry is events.

Have you worked events before?

Have you ever organized an event?

Have you ever operated an event?

Have you ever created a fundraising event?

If you don't have a lot of experience in running events, create your own fundraising event.

It might be a fundraiser that is very important to you or a fundraiser that's important to your family.

Perhaps it's a 5k walk, bowling, dance-a-thon; anything that requires you to get a sense of planning, digital marketing, and advertising. Selling sponsorships and executing is going to be a relevant skill set because all of those skills are transferable.

Let's recap multiple skills.

Sales, digital marketing, event management and content creation, graphic design, editing, and your social media channels.

How many followers do you have on your own channels?

You don't have to be an expert in all of it but understanding how they all stack together is very important.

"If you know how to sell, you like to sell and can close, you'll always have a job in sports."

Chapter 6

The Interview

How much value do you bring to an organization?

You have your education and you have multiple skills.

Now where's the value for the business?

"Well, I don't know if I really am in love with sales. I really like the marketing side, the social media, the digital media side.

I like operating events they are exciting, but I want to make more money. I should be in sales."

Don't try to do all of it, figure out what you really, really enjoy doing, and go all in.

Weaving up to that point will be forming your education to developing your skill sets, whether there's internships or relevant places that you are developing. If you're in your outside sales with the non-sports program, or you're doing operations for a different organization, agency, or non-profit group just make sure that these are skill sets that will be transferable.

Bringing value back to an organization.

Do you have a skillset that's better than anyone else's?

You really homed in on that skill set and it could be something like understanding CRM systems, or really good at Facebook advertising.

Become an expert in at least one area or prove you can execute.

Saying, "I'm passionate about sports," during an interview is a death sentence. At that point you should stand up, thank them for their consideration, and walk out the door.

Everyone who works in sports is passionate about sports. What makes you different?

Bring facts and value.

Employer: "Tell me about your experience."

You: "I started a website in college flipping sneakers to students at my school and online."

Employer: "Really, why did you start doing that business?"

You: "I always collected sneakers and when I would wear them to class, people would ask me where I bought them. I started to Snap and Instagram stories of whatever I was wearing or ones I wanted to flip, and it took off. Not only did I make $5,000 last semester but I have 10,000 followers on Instagram and Snapchat."

They never asked "sports management" experience, they only asked for experience.

Experience and skills come in many different forms. When you show your value of real life experiences, in this case building a business online and on campus, your knowledge, skills, and experience are all relevant.

Being industrious and entrepreneurial at a young age shows you have skills to start something and build it.

We live in a world where you need to be a participant to be noticed and the entry points are available to us all today. You don't necessarily need what may be deemed as relevant experience, interning and making coffee.

Build a following on YouTube or Twitter in an area you are passionate about, in or outside of sports. Manufacture and control that experience.

The employer will be impressed with action taken and being able to show results.

Don't be just a fan, become a participant in the business.

"The Greatest Day of My Life, Was My First Day at A Job I Always Wanted"

Chapter 7

Networking

It's not who you know, it's who knows you.

That's one of the most important things in business, and life, for that matter.

When I was growing up, I had an aunt who was the ultimate connector.

A tiny, proud Irish lady who smoked and drank like a sailor, told hilarious stories, and was always the center of every party.

She was very involved in local politics and volunteering for all the youth and high school sports in town.

Her house was in the middle of town and everyone would end up at it during the summer or holidays parties.

You never knew who would drop in. The mayor, a senator, the editor of the newspaper, a judge, or the head hockey coach.

That house was always buzzing with activity and, as you can imagine, I wanted to be there every day and never wanted to miss anything.

She didn't have any kids, so my sisters and I were considered her kids.

There was always a party, BBQ, or a penny poker game being played.

The house was always filled with coaches, kids, business owners, cast offs, and basically any character who she had in her vast network.

Funny thing was she was not rich, never held office, or owned a business in town.

She was a phone operator for New Haven Railroad. A job she had for forty plus years.

However, she had huge power in our community.

Why? Because everyone knew her, and she could introduce you to anyone.

I could hear her saying this line to me, which she said almost every day, at every party when people would leave, and we were cleaning up.

She said, "Rob, it's all about networking and connecting people together." She then followed with, "The top three most important things in business is what Rob?" I would say, "Networking, networking, networking."

She taught me that the ultimate power is in relationships. She would say, "you can get anything you need if you know the right people." She was 100% correct.

What are you doing now to network?

Now that you're out there looking for a job, you're banging on doors, you're hitting some walls, people aren't returning your phone calls, no one is returning your emails, or you had a couple of interviews, and you didn't get the job.

Chances are you had the interview on Skype or a phone call.

The problem is they don't know you or you don't know the right people to connect you to the decision maker or influencer.

Here's what you could do.

You can start by connecting with as many professors, guest speakers at your school, and start looking through their connections.

Who likes their posts? Reach out to those people.

Ask your connections to make introductions.

Reach out to industry executives you read about in Sports Business Journal or Front Office Sports and tell them you enjoyed that article they were in.

Connect with them on LinkedIn or Twitter. Or both.

Start engaging with their posts so they see who you are and start recognizing you.

You already complimented them. They are more willing to help a young professional or student than someone trying to sell them insurance.

So, there is a good chance they will accept your connect request.

If you feel that they are engaged with you and willing to help, ask them for 15 minutes of their time because you are impressed with their career. Tell them you would like to ask them questions because you're writing an article for your website, or on medium.com, and you just find their story and their journey interesting.

See what happens.

It's one of the greatest tricks, and it's how I got into podcasting, because I did just that.

I hit a wall with a client, or with a group that I heard was going to market on a special project.

I could not get a return email, or a phone call. I finally called and emailed this one gentleman that I knew who a very high-level gentleman in a major media group was. I asked him to do a podcast.

And that's what changed everything for me. He did it. He gladly returned that email quickly, and scheduled a time, which we did, and we ended by me being offered the RFP, which we were very excited about.

It all came about because I called up and I wanted to pick his brain. I wanted to ask him about his career for 15 minutes.

And ultimately, we built a little bit of a relationship, we built trust, I got in the door, and I was able to pitch some business.

So build that network up and create content if you can get that part of it. The most important thing is if you can create content that will grab the attention of employers and peers of organizations you wish to work for in the future.

Say you're stuck, you're not getting a job, or you're not getting the interviews that you want.

Start creating some content along those lines. You could write about your challenges, or you could write about your challenges of prospecting and looking for a job.

You could post, "Boy, I see this great opportunity for my favorite team and I know that this company is looking to do a great project with these types of sports."

#Hashtag the organization or people within the organization.

Write about it. Blog about it. Do a podcast about it.

Create the content to put it out there.

You may not necessarily be targeting exactly the organization that you want to talk to, the executives, or looking for a job with them.

What's better, doing nothing or putting it out there and trying to gain attention?

Maybe you could help somebody else.

Maybe the people you really want to reach saw what you put out there and remember your call or resume.

It's consistent repetition with content that is relevant. Especially on LinkedIn.

Maybe they'll remember your name the next time that you go and call that office.

So, the content that you're pushing out there is important to gain attention. Remember, you and thousands of others are going for very few jobs.

So, what is it that you're going to do that gets their attention? It's not going to be just a fancy phone call, or a fancy email, or something that you may send them.

It could be content that they read about out there. Unless you know who the owners are and unless you know who the decision makers are personally, you are in line for a job like hundreds or thousands of others.

You always want to be connecting with as many people that you work with once you get the job.

That networking is going to be so vital and so important for you.

And it's going to be building those relationships with the people that you work with, people that you work for, your peers, and people that work in different departments.

Have coffee with them, ask them about their jobs, ask them about their careers.

Volunteer for events outside of your department.

Maybe this is the department that you really want to work in, but there's no openings at the moment. Maybe you want to go in there and you want to volunteer to see if they need any help doing anything that might seem interesting to you.

Build those relationships. Build the network so that everyone knows who you are and ask them what you can do to help.

Let's recap.

The three most important things to remember is to: Network, network, network. Everyday find time in your day to fill in your schedule with quick coffees with colleagues and ask them for recommendations.

You want to see if you could ask them questions. You want to see if you could write an article about them.

If you're working for the company, you want to network as much as you can internally with people throughout the departments.

You want to network as much as you can with people on social media, especially people that you admire, as you become a student of the business.

And you want to continue to grow your network and build your relationships by helping others.

That's going to ultimately help you with your career.

So now that you've got your education, you've got your relevant skill set, you've got your experience, now you're building your network.

Now you're laying your foundation for your career.

You need to focus on your current job and do it better than anyone else. Regardless of how thankless that job may seem.

You don't want to be that old person who refuses to use social media.

You need to be willing to serve the cookies, which means, you need to be willing to serve others.

Being kind and helping others should never be below you.

Any level that you are working in a job, if you own the job and excel at it, you will not need a resume for your next step.

I use the expression, you have to be willing to serve the cookies, serve other people around you, your friends, your peers, your co-workers, and your staff that work for you, because it works.

Show them that you care rather than just saying it.

Stay on top of current trends and current events. Don't huddle in small groups and complain.

No one likes complainers. Be the one to stand above.

Be positive and nice to people. Be willing to do whatever you're asked. Don't gossip or complain. No one likes whiners.

Don't be that party person in the office. The person who is always running out to the bars or staying out late with people that you work with.

You don't need more friends at work. You have enough friends outside of work.

Always be the one to draw the line and be the first one to leave.

Don't be the party person, because at some point, those people may work for you.

Socialize when it's appropriate and be engaged when you do show up.

When you have conference calls and staff meetings, be prepared with updates on your work when you're needed.

Don't stare at your phone or computer. Pay attention, even if it's mind numbing and boring.

Know all the details in the area of your responsibility.

Don't ever ask and don't ever guess on something. Make sure that you know all the details within your responsibility and your scope of work.

Be prepared for meeting because that's when peers will evaluate your ability.

You prove them wrong when you're in a group setting and you know what you're talking about with confidence. You have confidence when you are prepared and know your stuff.

Then build a large network and strong relationships with your peers.

That's your foundation.

Your goal should be, if you have built a solid network foundation, you should never have to use another resume in your life, other than the first one.

Chapter 8

Find A Mentor

I was lucky enough to have amazing mentors along my career journey, but none made as big of an impact in my life both professionally and personally as much as Coach Tommy Groom.

I never played for Tommy, I met him after he retired and hired him to work for me at the NFL.

It was perfect timing as I was just starting out in my career and trying to figure how it all worked with a young family and very little business experience.

Tommy was one of those once in a lifetime characters you meet and if you read this all the way through you will be inspired and hopefully entertained as he had some crazy stories!

His advice to me on the day we met,

"Everything will fall into place, if you're headed to the right place."

This is Tommy Groom's story...

Tommy grew up in a very small town in what he liked to say, West "By God" Virginia. His blue collar, coal miner DNA, naturally allowed him to break down life into its simplest common-sense form.

He never made things overly complicated or dramatic.

Always looking for the good in people.

Tommy had a great college football playing career at Virginia Tech in the late 1960's and then spent the next thirty plus years coaching at the D1 level.

Like most coaches, he went through a gypsy life of transitions, packing up and starting over several times, and even being married several times.

The one thing I really admired about coach was that he never seemed to miss a day of living without maximum effort, a slick grin, and most important, that infectious positive attitude!

I can remember this moment like it was yesterday. I asked him, "Out of all the places you ever coached, where was the best time in your life?"

At that moment, this brilliant response forever changed my perspective.

"The best placed I've ever worked, is wherever I'm at."

He would tell me "Don't worry about your next job, make sure you are taking care of the one you're currently in."

Practical advice and 100% true.

Coach and I traveled around the world for several years operating the National Football League's Fan Development programs.

We put on hundreds of NFL youth events, camps, clinics, and tournaments from Boston to Bangkok. As you can imagine, we had the experience of a lifetime.

We were very lucky and we knew it. We never took the position or responsibility we had for granted.

We worked with incredibly passionate administrators, coaches, and players from all corners of the globe.

All though there were communication challenges, all of us had one shared goal; expanding a sport we all loved and having the platform to make a difference in kids' life through sports.

A natural bond.

Tommy and I spent thousands of hours together on planes, trains, in airports, hotels, on football fields, and occasionally in some of the wackiest places on the planet.

We were invited into countless homes of our host coaches to explore their culture and spend time with them and their families.

Even though we were tired from travel and long days running events, he pushed us not to miss a chance to discover new things and build friendships that have lasted twenty plus years.

He always said that no one really cares about how much experience you have or where you went to college. It's always about the relationships you build along the way that will be the single most import aspect to your career years from now.

He was spot on.

His thoughts on experience were summed up in this classic Tommy quote:

"You can no more do, what you don't know, to come back from where you ain't never been."

Let that one sink in.

Each trip was unique and special. We discovered how small the world really is and that there are so many generous, caring people in this world.

That was our common connector on every stop. We heard and shared amazing stories about overcoming obstacles and resources and how sports are a microcosm of life.

I shared a front row seat to listen and learn from all his incredible stories and was a participant on a great deal of new ones.

But I will never forget one of the many classic Tommy moments.

This one in particular was in Tokyo on a promotional tour for an NFL pre-season American Bowl game.

What Tommy liked to do out of respect for our hosts, would be to attempt to begin every press conference or event with a hello in the language of that country. Which they loved.

He usually gave me the task of helping him learn it on our way to each event. Sometimes I would have to remind him what country we were in, let alone learn a second language.

I would usually spend half the flight repeating how to say hello in whatever language over and over until he could finally say his standard greeting.

Sometimes I would be left to write the phrase on napkins. He didn't just look for my help. Typical Tommy would include everyone around him. He would practice on the flight crew, the people on the plane, and just about everyone in the airport, regardless if they were from the country we were traveling to or not.

I really do give him credit for trying, but he seldom got it right.

So this particular time in Tokyo, after practicing over and over on the eleven hour flight, we entered the press conference room. I looked him in the eyes and had him practice one last time, which he nailed.

I'm not sure what happened in the five seconds from the time he last practiced saying "Konnichiwa," to the moment he bowed, hit his head on the mic, looked at the crowd, grinned and said in perfect SPANISH… "Feliz Navidad!"

The room went dead silent. We couldn't believe what we just heard and the look on everyone in that room's face was a mix between confusion and sadness.

Until finally our Japanese interpreter respectfully broke the silence with a response of "Merry Christmas Coach". It was July.

Tommy had so many incredible stories and life lessons that were so out of this world crazy, but as I spent more time with him, I began to understand how, and more importantly why, they happened.

I could listen to his stories over and over again on our travels. They never got old.

The lessons of life he would weave into these stories were masterful and always relevant to what he knew was troubling me or anyone else we wound up meeting on the road.

His passion was people and he always had a way to put challenges into perspective, regardless if we were in South Korea or South Carolina.

A sad, but a legendary Tommy story, and the absolute moment when I knew he operated at a whole different level then the rest of the world, was from a phone call I received from him right after the New Years in 1998.

Although it was a very serious and a horrible event, his positive attitude was like a slap to the head. His character was truly revealed through the challenges he faced.

On January 2, 1998, I received that call from Tommy which revealed who he truly was.

Tommy: "Hey my man, I have good news and bad news."

I hesitated to ask, "Ok, what's the bad news?"

I kid you not, in a cool and deliberate voice he said, "My house burnt down!"

I was in shock. "How did that happen," I said.

He responded with a reason that I should have known, "Well, deep frying a turkey on my back porch!"

I was shocked and wasn't sure if he was fooling around. I asked, "Coach are you and the family ok?"
He said, "Yea we are all good, you know how quick I am on my feet. Got them all out safe except for the kids pet turtle, that thing was always too dang slow!"

Somehow, he found a way to let me know it's going to be alright.

We just cracked up.

I said, "Well if the bad news is your house burning down, what's the good news?"

Without missing a beat...he said, "We get a NEW HOUSE!"

So, one day after such devastation, he still found it in him to find the positive side of life during an incredibly sad situation for him and his family.

Sadly, they lost everything. The kids' Christmas presents, all their clothes, family photos and thirty years of championship rings, team pictures, and mementos that I am sure were very sentimental to his coaching career and life.

He found a way, which I'm sure was so painful, at the moment to find something positive out of this unimaginable event.

At the time, it obviously wasn't funny but as time passed and he sorted out his housing and got life back in order for his family, he would tell that very story with such gusto and detail, it too became part of his legacy.

He simply would never allow himself or anyone around him to act like the victim in any situation and was never looking for sympathy. He turned it into a lesson for all of us.

He lived his life exactly how he lectured so often about.

The funny thing was he never brought up that you should never cook a deep-fried turkey inside a covered porch attached to your house. That part was assumed by everyone.

When you did complain to him about challenges or people, he would always say, "If you can't roll with it, buy new tires."

I learned from Coach that it's all in your perspective on how to tackle a challenge you are facing. No matter how large or painful at that moment.

He would tell you to take a second, think about it, don't get emotional, and break it into common sense to find a solution.

He loved to say this about the tough decisions:

"Once you make a decision, it will be the best one you make."

He lived by the words he preached.

His zest for life, football, people, and enjoying the exact moment that he was living in, was contagious.

He believed that how you carried yourself was how others would perceive you.

He would sarcastically remark about naysayers, "I always have a chance to prove them right once I open my dang mouth!"

Regardless of the occasion, Coach was always the slickest dressed in the room.

He always wore a standard sport coat, polo shirt, jeans, and cowboy boots.

Out of our group of khaki and sneaker wearing schleps, he was the boss.

We would always tease him about his year round tan.

Which you should know, was only on his face.

I even asked him one time, "Why don't you ever tan anywhere else but your face?"

In Coach's simple, common sense he says, "My man, it only matters what you look like walking <u>in the door</u>."

Another life lesson learned, Coach!

Coach Tommy Groom passed away at the age of 55 in his sleep, March 2003. He was attending a coaching clinic doing what he loved. Helping and teaching others.

Coach had a major impact on all those who knew him, worked with him, lucky enough to be coached by him, and call him a friend, dad, brother, or even an ex-husband!

I was so incredibly fortunate to have spent all those years with him and honestly had never seen him mad or hear him say a bad word about anyone.

I do think of him often and the massive impact he has had on my life. Especially during trying times. What an incredible mentor.

I only wish I had an opportunity to say goodbye and thank him.

But I hope how I lived my life by always trying my best, helping others, staying positive and enjoying every moment is my thank you to Coach...wherever he's at.

Finding a few mentors can make a massive difference in your life and career simply because mentors have experienced life. Life lessons from your mentors are more valuable than anything you will ever learn in school.

"You can no more do, what you don't know to come back from where you ain't never been."

Coach Tommy Groom

10 Key Habits That Will Help You Have A Long Career In The Sports Industry

1. Volunteer

2. Stay connected to your colleagues

3. Be a student of the business

4. Always be positive, don't gossip!

5. Network, Network and Network

6. Start the week preparing on Sunday nights

7. Try every type of job as you can in the industry

8. Follow through on what you promise

9. Go All In on LinkedIn engagement and content

10. Find a few mentors

Career Development Actionable Check List:

1) Complete Self-Assessment www.gameplanu.org
2) Register for a career coach 90day program gameplanu.org
3) Make Your Social Media Channel Public & Clean it up!
4) Subscribe to www.frontofficesports.com
5) Start Blogging, Podcasting or start a Youtube channel
6) Connect with 5 new business contacts per week
7) Stay in contact with professors and mentors
8) Attend career webinars and networking events
9) Update Linkedin and have professional head shots taken
10) Schedule 1:1 Career Coaching Calls Gameplanu.org

Questions To Ask Career Coach:

_____
_____
_____
_____
_____
_____
_____
_____
_____
_____
_____
_____
_____
_____

Career Coaching 90Day Program

Session One:
Task:_____

Notes_____

_____

_____

_____

_____

Session Two:
Task:_____

Notes:_____

_____

_____

_____

_____

Session Three:
Task:_____

Notes:_____

_____

_____

_____

_____

All Rights Reserved 2019 ISBN 9781727603330

Made in the USA
Columbia, SC
07 November 2020